1 9 6 5

1 9 6 5

POEMS

J. R. SOLONCHE

SHANTI ARTS PUBLISHING

BRUNSWICK, MAINE

1 9 6 5

Published by Shanti Arts Publishing

Designed by Shanti Arts Designs

Cover images: (top left) AdobeStock [kokoshka]
(top right) AdobeStock [MI Sumon]
(bottom left) AdobeStock [kokoshka]
(bottom right) AdobeStock [kokoshka]

Shanti Arts LLC
193 Hillside Road
Brunswick, Maine 04011

shantiarts.com

Printed in the United States of America

ISBN: 978-1-971191-07-2

Library of Congress Control Number: 2026935638

Titles by This Author

Poetry

Vanity
The Consolations
Collected Short Poems
Barren Road
Night Visit
Old
Then Morning
Reading Takuboku Ishikawa
The Architect's House
God
The Eglantine
Alone
The Dreams of the Gods
The Book of a Small Fisherman
Leda
It's about Time
Around Here
The Lost Notebook of Zhao Li
Coming To
Life-Size
The Five Notebooks of Zhao Li
Selected Poems 2002–2021
Years Later
The Dust
A Guide of the Perplexed
For All I Know
The Moon Is the Capital
  of the World
Piano Music

Enjoy Yourself
The Time of Your Life
The Porch Poems
To Say the Least
A Public Place
True Enough
If You Should See Me
  Walking on the Road
I, Emily Dickinson
  and Other Found Poems
The Jewish Dancing Master
Tomorrow, Today and Yesterday
In Short Order
Invisible
Heart's Content
Won't Be Long
Beautiful Day
Peach Girl: Poems for
  a Chinese Daughter
  (with Joan I. Siegel)

Criticism

An Aesthetic Toward Notes:
  On Poets & Poetry

Contents

1965

It was 1965.
I dropped out of college.
I was 1-A.

So the letter came.
It was a greeting card from Uncle Sam.
"Greetings," it said.

So I went to Whitehall Street.
It was 5 AM.
It was dark.

It was drizzling.
It was dreary.
I was scared shit.

But I had the letter from Dr. Bearman.
It said I had albuminuria.
I don't know why Dr. Bearman thought that would get me out.

But it was all I had.
I recognized a few from high school.
Goldstein was there.

Weintraub was there.
Grazioli was there.
But he wasn't drafted.

He was there to join the Marines.
I had a clipboard.
I went from line to line.

I went from station to station.
I passed everything.
But I had my letter which I hadn't shown yet.

I didn't know which doctor to show it to.
Wasn't there a kidney doctor to show it to?
I was running out of doctors.

The last station was the eye exam.
"Take off your glasses and read the last line," the sergeant said.
I knew he was a sergeant.

I had seen sergeants in movies.
I recognized the stripes.
I took off my glasses.

I couldn't see the last line.
I couldn't see the chart.
I could barely see the wall.

"I can't read it," I said.
"Give me those glasses," the sergeant said.
I gave him my glasses.

He put them under some kind of microscope.
He shook his head.
He wrote "Z" next to my right eye.

He wrote "Z" next to my left eye.
"What does "Z" mean?" I asked.
"It means you're Zeed out," he said.

He gave me my clipboard.
"You're 4-F. You're fucking blind," he said.
"Thank you," I said.

So I didn't need Dr. Bearman's letter.
So I didn't need albuminuria.
So I didn't need a kidney doctor.

So I didn't need to go to Canada.
So I just needed my eyes.
So I thanked my father for his Z eyes.

So I thanked my grandfather for his Z eyes.
So I thanked my great-grandfather for his Z eyes.
So I thanked my lucky Z stars.

HUMMINGBIRD

Where are you now, ruby throated wonder?
I know somewhere north of Mexico
and south of my window, but where is somewhere?
It's late March, almost April, so you're at least
in Louisiana by now to make it here before May.
I've read that most of you travel 20 to 25 miles a day,
and some of you 100 miles in a single day.
I don't know if you are like most or like some,
but you needn't rush, you needn't hurry.
Your favorite hornbeam will be here.
The sugar water will be here in the glass feeder,
redder than the reddest tulip. Take your time.
Soon enough will I ask you to rush.
Soon enough will I ask you to hurry.
Soon enough will I ask you not to take your time.

ZHAO LI APPROVES

of poetry, but he
is sorry to say
that it is the poets
he does not approve of.

ZHAO LI PAUSES

to admire the first daffodils.
Of course, he will also admire
all the other daffodils, too,
but not as much. "Is that wrong?"
he asks the first daffodils. "No,
Zhao Li, that is right," they say.

ZHAO LI IS CONFUSED

by an essay about poetry
in which the critic calls for
"close reading of the text."
"Is there any other kind?"
Zhao Li laughs. "Well, yes,
there is if one is far-sighted,"
he laughs again.

ZHAO LI HEARS

a crow behind him.
"Thank you, crow, for
reminding me that
I have work to do," he
turns around to say.

DIRTY WINDOWS

I haven't washed
my windows
in two years.
Why should I?
I could wash
my windows
every day for
a year, and it still
wouldn't make
the world look
any cleaner.
Look at what
they have done.
They have ground
the world down.
Look at what
they have done.
They have ground
the dirt in. Just
look at what
the filthy bastards
have done.

A DREAM

In my dream, I remembered
what never happened but
what should have happened
for me to have a dream about,
yet it happened in my dream
as surely as though in life.
I remember when it wasn't
happening thinking, "This
should be happening.
This should be happening."

THEORIES

I have a theory of why
I don't have one.
It's simple.
I don't like arguing with myself.

A DIALOGUE BETWEEN ZHAO LI
AND HIS STUDENT

"What is the difference
  between prose and poetry,
  Zhao Li?" a student asks him.
"Prose flows while poetry flowers,"
  Zhao Li responds. "But *prose flows*
  rhymes, so doesn't that mean
  it's a poem?" asks the student.
"Very well. Let's start again.
  Stories flow while poems flower.
  Is that better?" says Zhao Li.
"Yes, that is better. Thank you,
  Zhao Li," the student says.
"You're welcome. Now run along
  and play," Zhao Li laughs.

APRIL

Jealous of the wild
cherry tree's snow-
white blossoms,
winter has dropped
its own white snow
blossoms on its
drooping branches.

ZHAO LI PAUSES

to look at the snow melting
by the side of the road. "Ah,
how swiftly all the snow of
cruel winter disappears into
the earth. Would this same
golden sun cause all the cruelty
and suffering in the world
to melt and disappear into
the earth just as swiftly," he
sighs. Then, remembering
that the cruel emperor still sits
on his throne, Zhao Li weeps.

WIND

The wild cherry tree
has just bloomed,
and already the wind,
stronger than any wind
has a right to be in April,
is stripping the petals,
and I'm thinking this
has to be some strange
sort of jealousy.

TO MY SNOW SHOVEL

Snow shovel, you did just fine,
old shovel, old pal of mine.
Yes, you're a little worn,
a little rough around the edges,
but you did what was asked
of you, old man, clearing
the way for this old man
right behind you. We've made
a good team all these years,
but I've known you long enough
to be honest with you now.
I've had enough of you, old
shovel. I've had enough of snow,
enough of the cold, enough
of winter altogether. I've had
enough, but I promise you this.
When I go south with the geese,
I will not leave you behind.
I'll take you with me, not to use,
of course, never that, but just
to have around to remind me
of the hardships we shared
in the snow and the windy cold
and the curses you endured alone.

PRIDE

I'm proud of you, old
man white-blossomed
wild cherry tree, not only
for out-staring winter's last
shot of April snow but for
being more snowy white
than ever.

POETRY

Not everything rises
to the level of poetry.

Some things must
descend to it.

A MYSTERY

What is this bee looking
for? Not the azalea, which
it has just bypassed. Not
the myrtle over which it has
circled and circled. Not
the daffodils to which it seems
totally oblivious. I will never
know unless I ask my neighbor
to whose yard it has flown.
Even then I will never know.
I know my neighbor. He's a good guy,
but he has no interest in bees.

ZHAO LI CONTEMPLATES

his seventy-ninth spring.
"Why do you look so smug,
Zhao Li?" the wild cherry
tree asks. "I have known
more springs in my lifetime
than most of the people—
all the billions and billions—
who have ever lived," he
answers smugly. "Ah, foolish
man. You will never know
your one hundred-fiftieth
spring as I now do, nor ever
know the ecstasy of blossoming,
not even once, nor ever know,
not even once, the gathering
of the joyful honeybees in
your hair," says the wild cherry
tree. Zhao Li sighs, for he knows
this to be all too true.

SPRING CONVERSATION

I asked my neighbor why
she feeds the birds all year.
"I want them to live all year
round. What do you do?" she
said. "I want them to live all
year round, too, but I stop
feeding them in May," I said.
She gave me a dirty look.
"They need to survive on
their own, without the crutch
of my help," I said. She kept
the dirty look. "You know,
they survived just fine before
we came along." She kept
the dirty look. "I feed them
during the winter, you know,
when it's hard for them,"
I said. She kept the dirty look.
"No problem. They'll come
here," she said through
a dirty little smile.

A QUESTION

What if we were like
the trees, and instead of
lying down when we die
and leaving, we remain
standing, gray and dry
and stiffly unalive among
the living trees leafing out
all around us as though
nothing had happened?
What if we were like that?

THEM OLD OLD-FASHIONED FASCIST BLUES

Oh, I've got them old old-fashioned fascist blues.
Yeah, I've got them old old-fashioned fascist blues.
My country's goin' down, right down, down the tubes.

Oh, I've got them old old-fashioned fascist blues.
Yeah, it's the same old old-fashioned fascist blues
from my hurtin' head right down, down to my shoes.

Oh, I've got them, old old-fashioned fascist blues.
Yeah, I've got them old old-fashioned fascist blues.
Everyday, everyday there's worse and worse news.

Oh, I've got them old old-fashioned fascist blues.
Yeah, it's the same old old-fashioned fascist blues.
They're goin' for folks of color, soon the Jews.

Oh, I've got them old old-fashioned fascist blues.
Yeah, it's them same old old-fashioned fascist blues.
Shit, they're even eyin' the National Zoo.

Oh, I've got them old old-fashioned fascist blues.
Yeah, I've got them old old-fashioned fascist blues.
Then after them—hear me now!—it'll be youse.

Oh, I've got them old old-fashioned fascist blues.
Yeah, it's the same old old-fashioned fascist blues.
Oh, Lawd, Lawd, what the hell are we gonna do?

ZHAO LI BENDS DOWN

to contemplate the spent
daffodils, which, nevertheless,
are still as tall, as erect as ever,
but now, struggling to keep up
their heads, pucker their shriveled
golden mouths to kiss the sun
one more time. Then he rises,
makes himself as tall as he can,
sighs, and kisses the sun.

TO A FRIEND WHO TOLD ME TO STOP
WRITING ABOUT HUMMINGBIRDS

Fine, I will stop after
this one, but this one, see,
is not about hummingbirds.
It's about you, Charlie.

HAIR SALON

The woman in the hair salon
was talking about the people
she knows who just died, all
women. "Don't you know any
men who died?" asked the hair
stylist. "You mean the husbands?
They all died years ago," the woman
said. "That's right, I remember you
told me," said the hair stylist. "Yes,
God's in His Heaven and all's right
with the world," said the woman.

SWAN

A swan is not swimming on
the lake. It is swimming
somewhere but not here.
I, too, am not here, for I am
swimming with the swan.

TWO DOGWOODS

How the dogwoods flower
at the right moment, just
after the magnolia and
the wild cherry have dropped
their silken pink petals and
are leafing out, adding
to the green backdrop
to highlight their milky white.

FLOWER GHAZAL

Middle English period is the earliest known use of *flower*.
Flower is a borrowing from French, *flur*.

There are more than 300,000 species of flowers.
Montsechia vidalii is the oldest known flowering plant.

The Middlemist Red Camellia is the world's rarest flower.
Wolffia globosa is the world's smallest flower.

Rafflesia arnoldii is the world's largest (3 feet across) flower.
The lotus is considered the world's most mystical flower.

Konohanasakuya-hime is the Japanese goddess of flowers.
Ralph Waldo Emerson: "The earth laughs in flowers."

Heinrich Heine: "Perfumes are the feelings of flowers."
A film (2012) with Paul Rudd is *The Perks of Being a Wallflower*.

    So, Solonche, any more to say on flowers?
    Not yet. Ask me tomorrow. I'm a late bloomer.

COIN GHAZAL

The word "coin" originates from the Latin word *cuneus*.
The ancient Kingdom of Lydia invented the first coins.

The 1849 Gold Double Eagle is the world's rarest (only
    one exists) coin.
The Uzbek tiyin is the world's lowest value (1000 = 1 penny) coin.

The 1804 Silver Dollar is the King of American coins.
Visitors to military grave markers commonly leave coins.

In Feng Shui, the farthest left corner of the room is where
    to put coins.
Sixpences have prompted more superstitions than other coins.

Patton Oswalt: "If you hit a midget on the head with a stick,
    he turns into 40 gold coins."
"Star Money" is a German fairy tale in which falling stars
    are transformed into silver coins.

In the movie, *Breathless* (1960), Jean-Paul Belmondo
    romances Jean Seberg with coins.
A meme coin is a cryptocurrency also known as shitcoin.

    So, Solonche, all finished with this ghazal about coins?
    I don't know. Shall we flip a coin?

KEY GHAZAL

According to Pliny the Elder, Theodorus of Samos
        in the 6th century BCE invented the first key.
Every key was unique until 1917 when it became
        possible to duplicate keys.

Twenty-eight feet two inches tall by 11 feet 4 inches
        wide is the size of the world's largest key.
Swedes say to cure whooping cough drink north-flowing
        brook water out of a church key.

In Greek mythology, Hecate is the goddess associated
        with keys, especially Hades' keys.
In some cultures, it is considered good luck to find
        an odd number of keys.

Sam Shepard, *True West:* "Give me the keys."
One Human Family is the motto of the Florida Keys.

A song by Cole Quest and The City Pickers (2021) is
        "Way Over Yonder in the Minor Key."
E flat major and C minor were Beethoven's favorite keys.

A great noir film (1935) starring George Raft is *The Glass Key.*
Alan Ladd, Veronica Lake and Brian Donlevy are in
        the remake (1942) of *The Glass Key.*

        So, Solonche, does this enigmatic ghazal have a key?
        Not at all. It's not a roman a clef.

ZHAO LI MEETS WANG WEI

on the road. "Wang, my old
friend, it has been such a long
time. How old are you now?"
Zhao Li asks. "We have not seen
each other in years, and the first
thing you ask me is how old I am,
Zhao Li?" says Wang Wei. "Yes,
but I will go first. I am 78," says
Zhao Li. "All right then, I am 91,"
Wang Wei says. "Do you have
advice for a 78 year-old man who
wants to live to be 91?" Zhao Li
asks. "Yes, be more polite to all
those you meet, especially
your elders," says Wang Wei,
continuing on his way.

AFTER DAYS

of gray and rain, Zhao Li goes
for a walk. The sky is clear
and blue. It is a simple sky
of simple blue. "It is true.
There is no beauty better
than a simple sky of simple
blue," he sighs, squinting up
at the sky, which at long last
is simple and blue.

THE ODDS

A dandelion seed drifts
its way to a dead end
at the end of my driveway
unless it finds, in a million
in one chance, a crack,
which is not unheard of.

HOME

Now it is part of the tree,
this old birdhouse,
weathered indistinguishably gray.
"Do not feel bad that the birds
no longer come. You are mine
now. Welcome home," says the tree.

AGAIN

While sitting outside again
waiting for the hummingbird
to appear at the feeder,
Zhao Li glimpses a cardinal
out of the corner of his eye.
"Thank you for reminding me
that not all that flashes red
are rubies," he laughs.

LIFE

So much life now in May,
here in the yard, here in the grass,
here in the wood adjacent to the grass,
so much pure and lively, living life, one
cannot believe that death was ever here,
all around and is, all around,
and will ever be, all around, so
since we cannot, then let us not, all around.

SAY

I just read "At the Faucet
of June." What is there to say
about it? What is there
to say about anything? Let us
say about everything, Always
the discovery, always the surprise,
always the utter belief in disbelief,
always, as you, Bill, would say,
and have, always under the spell
of underestimation.

TWO CLOUDS

When the two clouds came together,
one from the east, the higher one,
slowly, the other, the lower one,
from the west, slowly, they looked
like lovers in a slow-motion scene
of a tear-jerker, and it rained.

WIND

It comes out of nowhere,
crosses the road,
then goes back to nowhere,
leaving a trail of branches in its wake,
raging against invisibility.

KOAN BASED ON A FIRST LINE
BY EMILY DICKINSON

Soft as the massacre of suns,
say it. *Soft as the massacre*
of suns, again, intone again,
soft as the massacre (recite)
of suns far, far into the night.

MAY PASTORAL

The wind doesn't know its own strength.
The trees must shout to convince it.

The white irises surprise the peonies.
"Who are you?" ask the peonies.

The peonies surprise the white irises.
"Who are you?" ask the white irises.

A dragonfly is not greedy.
A dragonfly knows just how much sun it needs.

A hawk is not greedy.
A hawk knows just how much sky it needs.

The earth is not greedy.
It knows it needs the whole sky.

THE PEONIES

When the white peonies open,
stand and marvel,
for what else is to be done?
They are speaking, so listen, listen.
What more can you do?
They are telling you what white sounds like.

ZHAO LI FEELS

a pain in his lower back.
"Thank you, Pain in My Lower Back,
for reminding me that I'm an old man.
But am I a foolish old man or a wise old man?
The young call me Wise Old Man.
The old call me Foolish Old Man.
So I must be both a wise and foolish old man
and very often at one and the same time," he laughs.

DEAD BIRD

If I'm asked what happened,
I will not say it died because
it flew into the glass of the window,
nor will I say it died because
it was my window. No, if I'm asked,
I will say it died because it wanted
to fly in a sky that was not there.
That is what I will say if I'm asked,
the same as what I say to myself now.

CEMETERY

Every time I pass the old
family cemetery, I want
to pull over, get out and
walk around for a moment.
I never do, for there's nothing
to see, really. Just names
and dates, of which some
are still legible, most barely
so, and a few weathered
to nothing. The fact that
it's still here is enough.
I'll continue to pass by, and
I'll continue to respect them
by leaving them in peace,
the peace that is all they want,
that is all we ever really want.

NEIGHBORS

If we did not know any better,
would we not say that the irises
grew right here next to the peonies
to show them how to hold up
their heads, or that the peonies
grew here right next to the irises
to show them the meaning of humility?

TO ----

I have said the same
thing so many times
in so many different
words, I will have to fall
silent soon. You have
to admit, though, that it
was your fault for insisting
on the truth, which I did
as slanted as I could, in as
many different ways as
I could, but it seems none
was quite slanted enough
for the truth to slide straight
off and out of sight.

ZHAO LI MEETS

the poet Wang Wang.
"Did you read my poem,
Zhao Li?" asks Wang Wang.
"Yes, Wang Wang, I read
your poem three times,"
answers Zhao Li. "So what
do you think?" Wang Wang
asks. "I think three things,"
Zhao Li says. "I will tell you
the first thing now, I will tell
you the second thing tomorrow,
and I will tell you the third
thing the day after tomorrow,"
says Zhao Li. "And what is
the first thing?" "The first thing
is this—I do not like the poem.
Meet me tomorrow and I will
tell you the second thing."
"No, Zhao Li, I will not meet
you tomorrow, for I am going
to the North to visit my son."
"Very well then. I will tell you
the second and third things
now. I will not like the poem
you will write about going to
the North, and I will not like
the poem you will write about
returning home again," Zhao Li
says, waving goodbye.

ZHAO LI PAUSES TO SMELL

the honeysuckle, which stirs
in his mind memories of his
childhood. "Strange how
the fragrance of this honeysuckle
stirs up memories of my childhood.
We never had honeysuckle growing
at my childhood home. But we
must have, for now I remember it.
What else, oh, what else must
have I forgotten?" sighs Zhao Li.

MOVIE

The actress is not beautiful
but is beautiful. You know
the kind I mean, the kind that
act their way into the beauty
we expect of actresses, and
once have it, can hold it forever,
thereby typecast for their whole
lives like any other movie star.

ECSTATIC STATISTIC

If one in one hundred thousand
survives, can we not still
say it is ecstasy in
multiples of mystery?

HUMMINGBIRDS

Small but not frail
with a reputation
for ferocity I have
seen in action,
we should expect
no less from genes
that demand this
protectiveness.
Would our ferocity
be as spectacular.

NEWS ITEM: FATHER KILLS
ALL THREE DAUGHTERS

No, no, no—we are not
supposed to hear of such
things outside of Greek
tragedy as when Medea
murders her sons to take
revenge upon Jason
for his infidelity. No, no,
no—there is no Colchis,
not for this, not for this.

CURRENT EVENTS

I asked my friend Carol
if she needed anything,
for she was very busy,
overwhelmed actually
with work, and she said,
"A lobotomy. Do you need
anything?" "A one-way
ticket to New Zealand,"
I said, which was my way
of saying a lobotomy.

A CLOUD

A cloud is racing so fast across the sky,
surely it means it is running away
from something, surely it means something
is chasing it, surely it must be that its worst
nightmare is after it, surely it means cloud-death
is chasing it across the sky.

BECAUSE THE RAIN

has stopped, Zhao Li goes
outside to smell the world.
"The world smells new again,"
he says. "Yes, I do smell
new again, but don't be fooled,
Zhao Li. Your kind will befoul
me soon enough," the world says.
"I know, but not yet, not yet,"
Zhao Li says, inhaling deeply.

PEONIES

Spring was theirs.
It wore their colors.
Now they wither and droop.
Summer bangs at the door.
It smells of sweaty sweetness
and tramples on the path
of ten thousand exhausted
brown petals.

THE BUDDHA ON MY WINDOWSILL

has a big belly, a big cloth sack
on a stick over his shoulder,
a full bowl of rice in his hand,
and a big laugh on his face.
I, too, was fooled at first, but
later I found out that Budai's
belly was full of laughter and his
cloth sack was full of laughter
and his begging bowl was full
of laughter and that his laughter
was his way of teaching fullness,
so I laughed and was with fullness full.

THE RAIN

The rain gave what we asked of it.
It was generous, too generous.
It gave more than we asked of it.
Today it is enough. Today we ask it
to stop. Today we ask it to go away,
to bestow its blessing where it is
really needed, to a field parched,
to a lake too low, to a river crawling
on its knees, to a stream bed with
the ghost of water, to a reservoir
starving for attention. The rain gave
generously. It poured its heart out
to us. It is we who have the greener
pastures, who have the greener grass,
who are embarrassed to be so envied.

EARLY MORNING

Early morning,
and the trees look so
fit and trim in their early

morning green
and gold. They suit
them so well, the green

and gold of the early
morning like the spread
of a smile, serious and self-satisfied.

NOT LISTENING TO BACH

Whatever you
are listening to,
whatever you
are hearing,
if it is not Bach,
it is deafness,
just as whatever
you are looking
at if it is not
Rembrandt,
it is blindness.

A VERY BELATED LETTER TO ROBERT BLY

The first poet I wrote a letter
to was Robert Graves. He
didn't answer. That was 45 years
ago. It might still be in the Dead
Letter Office on Majorca.
The second was to A. R. Ammons.
I told him about my letter to Graves.
He answered. He congratulated me
on improving my taste. He sent
me an unpublished poem called
"Zero and Then Some." The third
letter is this one to you, Robert Bly.
Please don't tell me you're dead
and have been since 2021.
I won't hear it. I know you'll receive
this. You already have. I know
you'll answer. You already have.

WHEN

When I was ten, my mother
took me to the Metropolitan
Opera House to see *Carmen*.
We waited at the stage door
for the soprano, Rise Stevens.
She came out, smiled, took my pen,
signed my unrolled *Playbill*,
looked down at me, smiled again,
pushed her mink over her shoulder,
and got into her limousine.
I don't have her autograph anymore.
Only her long white legs disappearing
into the dark depth of the black car.

A MEETING

A deer steps out of the woods.
It looks at Zhao Li approaching on the road.
Zhao Li stops and looks at the deer.
They look at one another a long time.
It seems like a lifetime.
Then the deer darts back into the woods
beginning its new life.
Then Zhao Li continues on the road
beginning his new life.

SUNSET

A wind has come up at sunset
from the west and has pushed

me into the noise of the crickets
in the tall grass by the yews

and has pushed me across the road
into the mournful whistles of the two

owls whistling one owl to the other owl
in the wood's shadows. A wind has come

up and has pulled me from my foolish
preoccupations, and has pulled me from

the mourning of my two souls
whistling one soul to the other soul.

HOUSE AT DUSK BY EDWARD HOPPER

On the top floor of the apartment house,
(which is the only one we see in its entirety),
a woman is resting her arms on a windowsill.
She is looking down into the street below.
She is waiting for her husband to come home
from work, for it is dusk, and it is time for him
to come home. She is watching for him.
The sky is yellow. Between the sky and the roof,
the building is an unbroken mass of trees, green,
dark green, darker green, and in the deepest
recesses among them, darkest green to black.
To the right, barely in the picture, is a streetlamp
whose light is the sky's yellow. Two flights of steps
ascend a low slope and disappear into the depths
of the trees. It is darker there than the night that
is coming. Are we meant to follow them up
into the mind of the woman in the window,
watching, waiting for her husband to come home
as it is dusk and time for him to come home?
It is darker in her mind than the night that is coming.

WHAT THE DEAD SAID

The last passion is the passion to last.
This is what they said in my dream. They said,
We saw the future in the mirrored past.

We never believed it could be so fast.
Some sat in chairs. Some stood around the bed.
The last passion is the passion to last.

We never realized it in our haste.
Their voices dropped like stones from drooping heads.
We wanted more than just the mirrored past.

Beneath their feet was empty space, dark, vast,
cold, silent, terrible, terribly sad.
The last passion is the passion to last.

We lived for pleasure, heedless of the waste
until we made the waste of years our need.
We loved the future, and we loathed the past.

Their words were whispered breaths, mere wispy ghosts
of words. Their lips were brass. Their tongues were lead.
They said, *We lost the future, and we killed the past.*
They said, *The last passion is the passion to last.*

CITY PIGEON

Before she moves, I think she is a stone of snow.
She is all white, like a gull.
But her expression is not gull-like.
It is more benign, less self-assured.
Her eyes are black beads.
Her beak is the yellow of old piano keys.
Among her tail feathers, I see bad weather.
She has found a home on the sill of a boarded-up
window recessed beneath the overhang of the bodega.
Every minute or two, she drops down,
pecks among the small sticks,
picks one she likes and carries it up.
But I have seen boys here,
too small to reach that sill,
use a long stick they found under a hedge nearby,
to loose birds sheltered before down,
as though stones, into their hands.

NOTES FOR A LECTURE

Tell them it is a folktale.
The hero is a stranger in town.
They know how it goes.
He has a mysterious past.

He has a secret.
There is hunger in his eyes.
Between the stranger and the family,
there is suspicion, a bad taste.

But the stranger proves himself.
Prosperity returns to the house.
They know how it goes.
The stranger falls in love with the daughter.

She is lonely and sad and has
a great hunger in her eyes.
Tell them about the scene in the park.
Tell them about the snow, the moonlight.

Tell them about the attempted rape.
The daughter returns the gifts
the stranger gives her,
the black wool scarf with gold thread,

the leather Shakespeare
that falls to the floor one day,
open to Romeo and Juliet.
Do not comment on this.

Or say merely it is a lapse in taste
the author could not resist.
Tell them it is a folktale.
They know how it goes.

AESTHETICS

What is wanted is a regularity
of means
to ends of unforeseen
irregularity.

What is wanted
is a self-possessed routine
to uncertain ends,
in other words,

the spired city around
the next bend in the road.
What is wanted is the serenity
of pace,

the cadence of peace,
the possession of place, where
discovering—expecting
the voice—the face.

THE ROSE RABBI

The rose rabbi
was in love,
so he forsook
his dark study,
so he forsook
his dusty books,
and he went out
into the meadow.
The rose rabbi
went out into
the meadow to
gather flowers
and carried them,
great gatherings
of flowers, in his
arms back to his
dark study, back
to his beloved books.

THE SHADOW

I walk the street behind the shadow.
The shadow goes ahead of me,

avoiding other shadows
as urgently as I avoid others.

At the corner, I turn and stop
and for a moment,

leave the shadow alone
by the street lamp.

Now the shadow follows me.
Now the shadow enjoys the view,

the scenery, the passersby,
paying no attention to where it is going,

leaving all maneuvers to me,
all deft escapes.

THERE ARE TIMES YOU MUST WONDER

There are times you must wonder
what you would have done had you been there.

You would have run at the first foot on the step,
the knock, or fought right there at the door,

right then, or given in, meekly, gone with them
the way the rest went, like sleepwalkers.

And later, at the rail station,
you would have grabbed under an arm

for a gun, shot as many, him at least,
before you yourself were shot dead.

And still later, in one of the cattle-cars,
with no light, no air, no water,

no hallucinations of hope,
you would have taken off your glasses,

stepped on them, and with a shard of a lens, cut a vein.
And later than that you would have refused to eat,

given it away or let it be stolen.
You never would have lived, for that would have been a sin.

UNVEILING

It is March.
I am gathering wet,
cold leaves from their wintering in the flowerbeds.

The soil is frozen in places.
It is crusted with ice that cracks and splinters
as I peel the leaves from the dirt.

I think of my father.
I think this is the worst earth, the worst earth.
I think of my father while I kneel now in the earth
        so many leavings later.

I think of the cry my mother cried.
The cry my mother cried had a year of grief in it.
I remember how awkwardly I walked.

I remember how I stumbled over the Hebrew prayer.
There were stones in my mouth.
He deserved a walk steadier than my walk.

He deserved a prayer cleaner than my prayer.
He deserved better than that from an eldest son.
I think of the dirt on the shovel, the dirt that slid off the shovel,

that sliding of dirt from a shovel I heard in my sleep years after.
So long after, I feel the wet leaves through my gloves. My
hands were cold on the handle of the shovel
        those springs ago.

They are numb now and white.
They burn.
My hands burn as I sit, as I shiver.

WAR

It's really just a kind of dialogue, isn't it?
A sort of cowardice in reverse?

I say you are foolish,
and you say I am ignorant.

I say you are ugly,
and you say I am fat.

I pull the sleeve of your sweater,
and you poke me in the chest.

I say you are dead wrong,
and you say I am dead wrong.

And then hatred happens,
or anger without hatred,

or hardness without anger,
or stubbornness without hardness,

and I make a fist,
and you make a fist

until I am dead right,
or you are dead right.

EARLY ENGLISH

Today I learned that two
of the earliest words in English
are *town* and *priest,*
and I have been wondering
what a conversation between
two of the earliest Englishmen
might have been like.
Perhaps they talked about
going to town to see the priest.
Or going to the priest to get
his blessing before going to town.
Or having the priest bless
the ground where they were going
to build a town. Or hearing the priest,
in his sermon say that the town
is a place of sin, a Sodom,
and they ought never set foot there.
In the country, one might say,
while gesturing, *Town priest.*
In town, one might say, while
gesturing, *Priest town.*
And surely many other words
would have to be invented.
Words like *father* and *confession.*
Words like *let's* and *go* and *to.*
Words like *sorry* and *mate* and *can't.*
Words like *because* and *I'm* and *broke.*
Words like *damn* and *wife.*

GOD

I had a dream about God.
It was a country estate.
He was in the library.
It was a warm room,
richly paneled in dark wood.
There were leather chairs,
a large desk and floor-to-
ceiling shelves of books.
He was standing, looking
out the window. It was dusk.
The sunset was beautiful.
He was tall and rather thin.
He was dressed in evening
clothes. But the black bow
tie was undone, and the collar
was unbuttoned. He held a
drink in his hand. It was the
best bourbon. He was parting
the curtains with the other hand.
He was about sixty years old.
He knew I was in the room
a long time before he spoke.
"I am either the greatest of all
liars or simply the lie itself.
I do not know which." I liked
his voice. It was soft. It was like
a woman's voice. I wanted to say
something. I was actually just
about to, but he turned his back
and lifted the glass to his lips.
I knew he didn't want me to say
anything. I knew he wanted no
pity, no sympathy. I knew he

knew that this was the price he
had to pay for being who he was.
So I turned around and left him
to the universe of regrets that
were his only memories.

IN THE SHADOW

of the Chateau Frontenac,
I bought a poem.
It was printed in French
on a small pink card.
It was about the poet's loneliness
and his despair.
It was about the only friend
he has, whose name is Jesus.
The poet was in a wheelchair.
His body was contorted.
His speech was slow
and barely comprehensible.
It was not a good poem.
In fact, it was very bad.
But I wept after reading it there.
And this is something I have never done.
Not after Wordsworth or Keats.
Not after Whitman or Dickinson.
Not after Basho or Beaudelaire.

MORRIS KARP

Morris Karp was born in Russia.
Morris Karp was the father of my mother.
Morris Karp came to America in 1910.

Morris Karp spoke only Russian
Morris Karp learned English in America.
Morris Karp got a job operating a sewing machine in America.

Morris Karp made pockets for businessmen's jackets in America.
Morris Karp made pockets for businessmen's coats in America.
Morris Karp knew injustice in America.

Morris Karp did not know the word *injustice*.
Morris Karp was active in the union of garment workers.
Morris Karp fought for a 40-hour week.

Morris Karp fought for decent conditions of work.
Morris Karp fought for a living wage.
Morris Karp was beaten by a police officer on the street.

Morris Karp showed me the scar he got in America.
Morris Karp showed me the perfect pockets he made in America.
Morris Karp told me something.

Morris Karp told me how he learned the difference between
    tear and *tear*.
Morris Karp said, *A tear is a tear in your eye.*
Morris Karp said, *A tear is a tear in your pocket.*

SHORT JULY PASTORAL

A songbird vocalizes on the birdhouse roof.
At least it's still a songbird.

The breeze turns the page of my book.
The breeze is certainly wiser than I.

A fence-high dragonfly has enough sky.
Wasps nest next to the hummingbird feeder.

The last evening primrose withers.
There are no flowers in this desert of green.

#1670

Emily, Emily, Emily, your one
thousand-six-hundred-seventieth
poem is such a strange poem, even
for you, Mistress of Strange Poems.
It is the one in which you come
upon, in a dream as you say, a worm,
"pink, lank, and warm,"
which you leash with a piece of string
to your bedpost to keep it from wandering.
You leave for a while, and when
you return later, you find the worm
transformed into a snake, but "ringed
with power." You interview
the worm-snake until it fathoms you.
Yes, Emily, that is your word, "fathoms."
And then you run out of the room
and out of the house and out of town,
only to claim, in the very last line,
as I said before, "This was a dream."
Mistress of Strange Dreams, I'm not so sure.
Mistress of Slant, I wonder.

THE MOVIE OF THIS POEM

For the movie of this poem,
I want James Dean
and Martin Sheen
to play the masculine
rhymes. For the feminine
rhymes, I want Bridgette Bardot
and Marilyn Monroe.
For the role of the accented
syllables, I want Richard Burton.
John Gielgud must play the caesuras.
I don't know about the music,
but Ingmar Bergman or
Stanley Kubrick will have to direct.
Never mind all that.
A silent film.
In black and white.
With Chaplin and a dog.

ZHAO LI PAUSES

to feel his age get worse.
It troubles him, for when
he was a young man, he
believed that aging would
make his age feel better.
He should have listened to
his grandfather. "Grandfather,
I should have listened to you.
Forgive me," mutters Zhao Li.

WOKE

My friend Jeff asked me
if my life had ever been
threatened. "Well, lots
of people have told me
that they'd kill me," I said.
"No, not like that. For
real," he said. "No. Were
you?" I said. "Yeah, twice,"
he said. "No shit," I said.
"Yeah, and both times by
dykes," he said. I know it
wasn't a joke, but we laughed
harder than either of us had
laughed in years.

ZHAO LI PAUSES

to consider why he pauses
so much. He laughs.
"Of course, that is where
the laughter fits!" he shouts
as he continues on his way.

AMERICA

Now it has happened. We are broken.
How quickly it happened. How quickly
the state of things has become the things
of state. It has happened. It is here. We
are broken. It can be ignored no longer,
cast no longer to attention's periphery,
to priority's margins. History has a new
meaning. It means today. It means this very
hour. History is broken. It repeats. Did not
our fathers warn us of this? Did not their
fathers warn them of it? Did not they warn
how history repeats? They did not learn.
It repeated. We did not learn. It repeats.
It is broken. Who is he? Who is this man?
Who is this child we put in charge? Who is
this breaker of the things of state? Who is
this breaker of the office's oath? Who is
this breaker of all vows and promises? Who
is this breaker? He is broken. Who broke
him? Did his mother break him? Did his
father break him? Who taught him how to
break the things of state? Who taught him
what to break? From whom did he learn it
so well? Breaking everything is all he knows.
Breaking everything is all that enlivens him.
Breaking everything is all that makes him
whole. Who are these who praise him? Half
the state praises him. What is half the state
that should praise the breaker? Is he breaking
them, those who praise him? No, they were
already broken. No, they were already beaten
down and broken. It is here. It is broken, broken

everywhere we look. Everywhere, everywhere
we look, all, all is broken. The state is broken.
It lies broken all around us. We know not where
to put our feet.

photo: Emily Solonche

Nominated for the National Book Award, the Eric Hoffer Book Award, and nominated three times for the Pulitzer Prize, J. R. Solonche is the author of more than forty books of poetry and coauthor of another. He lives in the Hudson Valley.

SHANTI ARTS

NATURE ▪ ART ▪ SPIRIT

Please visit us online
to browse our entire book catalog,
including poetry collections and
non-fiction books on nature, healing,
art, and more.

Also take a look at our highly
regarded art and literary journal,
Still Point Arts Quarterly, a feast for
the eyes and the imagination —
available to download for free.

www.shantiarts.com

www.ingramcontent.com/pod-product-compliance
Lightning Source LLC
Chambersburg PA
CBHW022110050726
47591CB00002B/751